BREAKING THE
ICE

BREAKING THE
ICE

How To Improve
Your On-The-Spot
Communication Skills

Deborah Shouse

SkillPath Publications
Mission, KS

Editor: Kelly Scanlon
Cover Design: Rod Hankins and Lisa Freeman
Page Layout and Design: Rod Hankins
Page Layout: Dave McCullagh

Library of Congress Cataloging-in-Publication Data

Shouse, Deborah, 1949-
    Breaking the ice : how to improve your on-the-spot communication skills / by Deborah Shouse.
        p.   cm.
    Includes bibliographical references.
    ISBN 1-878542-42-7
    1. Business communication.   2. Business presentations.   3. Nonverbal communication (Psychology)   4. Success in business.
    I. Title.
    HF5718.S52   1994
    302.2—dc20   94-2294
                                                                      CIP

        4   5   6   7   8   9   0   99   98   97

Printed in the United States of America

CONTENTS

Introduction 1

1 What Is Your "Ice Q"? 3

2 Ice-Breaking Body Builders 21

3 Lines That Melt the Ice 31

4 Listening Is Hot 49

5 Iceberg Alert: How to Deal
With Indifference or Rejection 61

6 Ice-Break While You Wait 67

Ice-Breaking and Business-Building Journal 77

Bibliography and Suggested Reading 79

EXERCISES

Exercise 1: What Is Your Current "Ice Q"? 5

Exercise 2: When I Glow 9

Exercise 3: Where I Need to Grow 12

Exercise 4: Warm Hearts and Cold Shoulders 15

Exercise 5: Fear Not 17

Exercise 6: Tuning In to Your Body Language 22

Exercise 7: How to Be Some "Body" 25

Exercise 8: Assessing Your Opening Lines 33

Exercise 9: Creating Your Own Grand Openings 39

Exercise 10: Creating Fiery Responses to Stale Questions 43

Exercise 11: Practicing Metaphorical Thinking 45

Exercise 12: Listen Up! 51

Exercise 13: How Much Listening Leverage Do I Have? 54

Exercise 14: Pulling Off Listening Leeches 58

Exercise 15: How Well Do I Handle Icebergs? 63

Exercise 16: Rebuilding the Titanic 65

Exercise 17: Your Own Ice-Breaking Situation and Solution .. 74

Introduction

*Y*ou've been in this situation before: You're waiting with strangers at an elevator, a reception area, a luncheon table. The silence is thick. You look at your shoes and notice their scuffs. You examine a splotch on the opposite wall. You search your mind desperately for something to say.

What you need are the skills to manage conversation at a moment's notice. You need to know how to instantly melt the ice and dispel the chill. You need these skills and you need them right away.

Why? Because these are the skills that make people remember you, feel comfortable around you, seek you out. These skills translate into increased confidence and effectiveness at work, at home, and in social situations. These are the skills that will help you turn those uncomfortable idle moments into business potential.

Breaking the Ice contains quick, easy-to-read chapters packed with practical information that teaches you how to:

- Bolster your self-confidence in uncomfortable situations.
- Tune in to other people's body language and help you become aware of the message you're sending with your own.
- Increase your listening acumen.
- Use ice-breaking skills to smooth conversational waters.
- Become a leader in new and unfamiliar situations.

Ice breaking can add richness to your life. You'll feel the power of your newly developed communication style and feel comfortable approaching people. Most important, you'll see your business opportunities grow as you seize these situations to make new contacts or gain valuable information.

This how-to book is a starting point for developing your ice-breaking skills. The exercises are designed as "hands-on" tools for putting the concepts you learn to work immediately. You'll also find summaries of ice-breaking techniques and tips throughout the book. Finally, after you've read through the book, keep it handy for a quick reference and review whenever you approach an ice-breaking situation.

One

What Is Your "Ice Q"?

*B*arry *is nervous about going to the job fair with his broken foot. Instead of his usual polished wingtips, he sports an oversized baby blue walking shoe and a cane. Walking is an effort. Barry feels embarrassed and unprofessional as he hobbles toward the convention center. Just as he nears a group of recruiters, he drops his briefcase. A well-dressed man picks it up for him.*

"What happened to your foot?" the man asks.

Barry tells him the story and the man asks questions. Soon they are deep in conversation. The man is looking for someone to work with him. Barry ends up getting a job he loves, working for this man.

Barry's story is a great example of how ice breaking can better your life. Ice breaking can inform, entertain, connect, and advance you. Of course, on-the-spot conversations don't always lead to a great connection such as a new job. Reaping these types of benefits usually takes many contacts and lots of time. But with each encounter, your confidence grows, helping you achieve communication skills that count.

In this chapter, you'll:

- Learn your ice-breaking style.

- Analyze your comfort zones (the situations in which you feel comfortable ice breaking).

- Discover tools for dissolving some of your communication barriers.

To get started, try Exercise 1. You'll learn your current "Ice Q"— how you typically react in ice-breaking situations.

Exercise 1

What Is Your Current "Ice Q"?

Are you an Ice Skater, Icebreaker, or Ice Melter? Take this quiz to find out. Circle the response that comes closest to the way you'd respond in each situation.

1. You're waiting for the elevator and it's taking forever. A man dressed in a conservative business suit is standing with you. The orange leather briefcase he carries presents an interesting contrast to his dark suit. What do you do?

   A. Tap your foot and hope the elevator hurries.

   B. Press the elevator "up" button again and give the man a controlled smile.

   C. Say: "What a brightly colored briefcase! What's the story behind it?"

2. Your appointment was for 2:00 p.m. and already it's twenty minutes after. The reception area has stiff, formal chairs and tables covered with neat stacks of the *Wall Street Journal, Forbes,* and *Fortune.* A woman strides in and sits on the opposite end of the sofa you're seated on. What do you do?

   A. Scoot closer to your side of the sofa, read the front page of the *Wall Street Journal,* and wonder why being on time isn't everybody's priority.

   B. Say "How are you?" to the woman and pick up a *Forbes.*

   C. Observe the woman, looking for conversation openers.

3. You don't know a soul at this business luncheon. You pick a seat at one of the tables for eight. Three people are already seated, each of them studiously reading the

program. One of them glances up and nods to you. What do you do?

  A. Pick up the one-page program description and act as though you're extremely interested in every word.

  B. Take off your jacket and say to the person next to you, "It's warm in here, isn't it?"

  C. Take a quick look at the program and say to the person who nodded to you, "Which of these speakers have you heard before?"

4. You feel as though the afternoon portion of the workshop will never end. You're finding it difficult to concentrate, and you want to hang a "Closed" sign over your eyes.

   During a break, you join the long line at the coffee machine. Behind you, two women are criticizing the workshop planners.

   "Why is the meeting room so cold?" one asks.

   The other adds: "And the sound system is poor."

   You haven't really noticed the room temperature or the sound quality.

   In front of you, two men are talking about last night's ballgame. "That coach is all wet," one says. The coach is a friend of your ex-sister-in-law's. You feel like you're being assaulted by negativity on all sides. What do you do?

  A. Examine the money you're holding and wonder whether the coffee will keep you awake the rest of the afternoon.

  B. Wait until there's a pause in the men's conversation and say, "Do you think this will end on time?"

  C. Smile at the women behind you, wait until there's a pause in their conversation, and say: "I overheard your concerns about this workshop. What are some workshops that you really liked?"

5. You're a few minutes early for a new client meeting. The receptionist who takes your name is a friendly-looking man. His nameplate reads "Devin O'Day," and there's a

troll statue on the corner of his desk. The reception area is empty. What do you do?

    A. Sit down and look for a magazine to read.

    B. Say to the receptionist, "Nice day, huh?"

    C. Say: "That troll adds to the atmosphere. Do you have time to tell me the story behind it?"

Now, how do you add up in the ice-breaking business?

Every "A" answer you chose means you felt uncomfortable tackling the situation. You're an "ice skater."

Every "B" answer means that you were willing, but lacked the confidence to make it happen. You're trying to be an "icebreaker," but you're not melting much ice yet.

"C" answers indicate that you chose to be an icebreaker. If you chose all "C" answers, you're a natural at ice breaking. You're a real "ice melter."

Did you have a combination of "A," "B," and "C" answers? Don't be surprised if you did. Each of us has situations where we feel comfortable breaking the silence and those where we don't. Few people naturally feel comfortable walking into every situation and taking charge.

Now that you know your "Ice Q," you can analyze the results. By learning what your own areas of comfort are and working within them, and then gently expanding those areas where you feel tentative, you'll improve your ice-breaking abilities, or your "Ice Q." By working on your strengths, you'll get stronger. Consider Ron in the story that follows:

> *Ron walks to the center of the stage and seizes the micro-phone. He smiles at the audience of managers and begins to tell a story: "In a time long ago, there lived a CEO much like the one who rules your own kingdom . . ." Ron weaves a tale that links the work world with a mythical Persian kingdom. Throughout the twenty-minute story, the audience sits transfixed, listening intently. When Ron finishes, the applause is deafening.*
>
> *"Great job," the meeting planner says when Ron leaves the stage. "Now I'd like to introduce you to a couple of people."*

"I don't know," Ron says. *"I'm not really good at meeting people."*

Ron is totally at ease in front of a large group, but his throat lumps and his hands grow sticky at the thought of meeting someone new one-on-one. You, too, have conversational areas where you shine and other areas where you'd like to watch the proceedings from a tall tree. Analyzing your strengths helps you progress in your quest for smoother interaction with new people.

Take a few minutes, close your eyes, and envision a specific time — a work or personal experience — when you felt calm, good, in charge of a situation that involved meeting new people. What kind of people were around you? What was the physical environment? What did you do to make yourself feel at ease? How did others feel about you? Try to see the exact setting and hear the conversations that went on. Then complete the "When I Glow" exercise.

Exercise 2

When I Glow

1. Describe a situation in which you felt comfortable meeting someone new. Be as specific as possible.

_____

_____

_____

_____

_____

_____

2. Who was there? Were they business associates, family members, social acquaintances? How many people were there? Did you know anyone?

_____

_____

_____

_____

_____

_____

3. Describe the physical environment (indoors, outdoors, large room, small room). Was food served? Were you seated or standing? Was the room temperature comfortable? Describe the noise level.

_____

_____

_____

_____

_____

4. What did you do to make yourself feel at ease?

_____

_____

_____

_____

_____

_____

_____

_____

5. How did you interact with people? What were the elements that made you feel so successful?

_____

_____

_____

_____

_____

_____

_____

_____

6. Now make a quick list of words that describe how the experience made you feel (e.g., empowered, calm, interactive).

_____

_____

_____

_____

_____

_____

_____

_____

7. Use these words along with your responses to the previous questions to create one sentence that describes ice-breaking situations in which you already feel at ease.

For example: "Ice breaking is easy when I feel empowered and I walk into a small room with a low noise level and only a couple of people."

_____

_____

_____

_____

_____

_____

_____

_____

Now you have a handle on the situations where you feel comfortable breaking the ice. But sometimes you pick the wrong people or situations or use the wrong tone of voice, and the world seems like a tiger about to pounce on you.

Think of a situation where you felt underwater, drowning, unable to breathe or think. Then use Exercise 3 to describe these areas where you need to grow.

Exercise 3

Where I Need to Grow

1. Describe your nightmare situation, a time when you
   tried to connect with new people and it didn't work. Be
   as specific as possible.

   _____

   _____

   _____

   _____

   _____

   _____

2. What kinds of people were there? Were they business
   associates, family members, social acquaintances? How
   many people were there? Did you know anyone?

   _____

   _____

   _____

   _____

3. Describe the physical environment (indoors, outdoors,
   large room, small room). Was food served? Were you
   seated or standing? Was the room temperature comfortable? Describe the noise level.

   _____

   _____

   _____

   _____

   _____

4. How did you interact with people? What made you feel so uncomfortable?

_____

_____

_____

_____

_____

5. If you could relive this situation, what would you do differently?

_____

_____

_____

_____

_____

6. Now make a quick list of words that describe the experience (e.g., angry, scared, sick).

_____

_____

_____

_____

_____

7. Using these words and your responses to the previous questions, create one sentence that encapsulates an ice-breaking situation in which you feel "out of your element."

   For example: "Ice breaking is difficult when people seem disinterested and occupied with other things."

_____

_____

_____

_____

Taking a Closer Look

You've analyzed an ice-breaking situation in which you shined and one in which you desperately wished Scotty had "beamed you up." Now you're ready to build on what you learned about yourself in exercises 2 and 3.

Reread your responses to the "When I Glow" worksheet in Exercise 2. Notice the types of people and the types of settings that put you at ease. These are the situations in which you feel comfortable ice breaking. Then reread your responses in Exercise 3 and notice the types of people and situations that challenge you. These are the mental battles you will be winning as you become familiar with ice-breaking techniques.

Now fill in the "Warm Hearts and Cold Shoulders" worksheet in Exercise 4. The more you understand your areas of strength and challenge, the better equipped you will be to achieve your full potential when you find yourself in ice-breaking situations.

Exercise 4

Warm Hearts and Cold Shoulders

Warm Hearts

List the types of people and environments you already feel comfortable with. What other types of people can you add to the list? What other environments? Brainstorm with yourself or with a friend and add to your list.

_____

_____

_____

_____

_____

_____

_____

_____

_____

Cold Shoulders

These are the situations in which you feel frozen, unable to be fluid and natural. To begin, write down the situations you listed in Exercise 3. What similar types of people and occasions have you struggled with?

_____

_____

_____

_____

_____

_____

_____

_____

Dissolving Your Communication Fears

"I'm worried they'll laugh at me."

"I'll say something, and everyone in the room will look at me as though I'm crazy."

"I'll talk to the woman waiting at the elevator, and she'll look at me like I'm mud on a white sofa."

Most people are followers waiting for a leader to arrive. And what better place to hone your leadership skills than in those otherwise wasted moments, during those times you spend waiting, those moments that tie together the day while you're rushing from meeting to appointment to seminar? Simply opening a conversation puts you in a leadership role.

Being a leader, even in something as seemingly innocuous as a three-minute conversation, takes courage. It requires the hacking down of old barriers and the dissolving of old fears.

"Wouldn't it be wonderful if we got up and met some-one," Judy says to Cindy as they wait for the finance seminar to begin.

Although Cindy agrees, neither of them stirs. Neither of them risks the awesome walk across the room to approach a stranger.

Why?

Stronger than any sentry, louder than any alarm bell, more powerful than an armed tank, FEAR stands in their way. How can you move such an insidious force out of your way?

By acknowledging your fears and writing them down.

Writing your fears down makes them concrete and manageable. Instead of some large amorphous thing roving through your head, they are small, concrete words on a piece of paper.

When you see your fears on paper, they may seem silly or juvenile. But don't edit them. Write down every one that floats into your mind.

Exercise 5

 Fear Not

Simply take one deep breath. Then write about your fears for at least five minutes. Write whatever comes to mind.

For example:

- "I fear disapproval."
- "I fear people making fun of me."
- "I fear rejection."

Things I fear about ice-breaking situations:

1. I fear . . .

_____

_____

2. I fear . . .

_____

_____

3. I fear . . .

_____

_____

4. I fear . . .

_____

_____

5. I fear . . .

_____

_____

6. I fear . . .

_____

_____

7. I fear . . .

_____

_____

8. I fear . . .

_____

_____

9. I fear . . .

_____

_____

10. I fear . . .

_____

_____

11. I fear . . .

_____

_____

Others:

_____

_____

_____

After you have spelled out your fears, take another deep breath. Read your fears aloud to another person. Listen to your voice as you read. Each time you acknowledge your fears, you become stronger.

Do this exercise as often as you need to. When you're finished writing down your fears, crumple up your paper and throw it on the floor. This reminds you that you don't need fear any more.

Things I Learned About Myself in This Chapter

1. _____

_____

2. _____

_____

3. _____

_____

Things to Do to Improve My Ice-Breaking Skills

1. _____

_____

2. _____

_____

3. _____

In this chapter, you learned your ice-breaking style, analyzed your situational comfort zones, and found tools for dissolving some of your communication barriers.

Your goal is to hone your on-the-spot communication skills so that regardless of your mood and circumstance, you'll shine in all your new situations. Working through this chapter has already put you a step ahead of the game.

Chapter

Two

Ice-Breaking
Body Builders

Gerri, a travel agent, makes it her business to notice other people's body language.

"Even in the grocery store line, I watch people. If they angrily flip through the magazines, if they fidget with their groceries, then I say, 'You look like you could use a vacation.' Often their faces flood with relief."

That simple icebreaker has really paid off for Gerri. One woman even ended up using her to book a dream trip to Hawaii!

Even when you're not saying a word, your body—through facial expressions, mannerisms, gestures, and posture—is communicating with the people around you. Is your body saying what you want it to say? Is it helping you make new contacts, or is it standing in your way? In this chapter, you'll learn tips on creating body-building language that will strengthen your ice-melting abilities. To begin, take a few minutes to complete Exercise 6.

Exercise 6

 ## Tuning In to Your Body Language

Circle the response that comes closest to the way you'd respond in each situation.

1. You've arrived for your last meeting of the day. But there are no chairs left in the reception area, so you stand. You plunk down your briefcase, fold your arms across your chest, lean against the wall, and close your eyes.

   Your mind is saying, "Won't somebody please be nice and offer me a chair?" But what is your body saying?

   A. "Back off, buster."

   B. "I'm shy but would like love and approval."

   C. "Talk to me, baby."

2. As you wait for your requisition, you begin talking with the clerk. She is telling you, quite volubly, about her prize zinnia garden. You stand with your legs a comfortable distance apart and your arms by your side. You lean slightly forward.

   You are thinking: "I wish my requisition would get here. I feel like I'm about to start sprouting." What is your body saying?

   A. "That's fascinating. I'm eating up every word. Tell me more."

   B. "I wish I weren't so tired. Could you talk more slowly?"

   C. "If you say one more word, I'm going to upturn the rubber plant in the corner."

3. You're waiting in a government reception area. The woman next to you begins talking about her teenage son.

"Sonny is the perfect child," she tells you. "He goes to church twice a week, he helps me with the house-work..." Your own teenager is probably at this moment watching soaps and drinking diet soda. Housework is an alien concept to him. You nod your head and cross your ankles.

Your mind is saying, "Maybe if I'd given Dan more chores when he was younger, he'd help around the house too." What is your body saying?

   A. "Is she telling the truth? Is this kid for real, or an escapee from *Leave It to Beaver?*"

   B. "I don't believe your story."

   C. "Isn't it wonderful that the American family is alive and well in your household?"

4. You are waiting in line for a table at a popular restaurant. The man beside you starts talking about the key to business success. He has recently taken a course in firewalking and believes that if everyone could just get up the courage to run across burning coals, the economy would be in better shape. "That's fascinating," you say as you pick a piece of lint off your jacket. Then you notice more lint.

"Yes," the man continues, "everyone, from entry-level people to CEOs, needs to do this." You hope he doesn't notice your lint patrol.

Your mind is saying, "I wonder if I'd have the guts to firewalk." What is your body saying?

   A. "I disapprove of your simplistic theory."

   B. "You're sticking your foot in your mouth, ashes and all."

   C. "I can't wait to try that for myself."

As you can see from Exercise 6, the mind nibbles at politeness, wants to be approving and good, but the body often blares forth its own statement.

Answer A is what your body is shouting while you're often thinking other things. Remember, nonverbal gestures carry more weight than words.

Although body language can be a complex and intricate art form, you can easily learn the basics. One of the most important things to remember is to take gestures in the context of their surroundings. A man with his arms hugged around his chest in 30-degree weather is not necessarily defensive. He may just be cold!

Here are some of the body cues to watch for when you're in an ice-breaking situation.

Face Facts

Your expression creates an opening or a barrier for the new contact. A smile sends a universal welcome.

But a hand-to-mouth gesture indicates a covering up, an untruth. Talking with your hand over your mouth indicates that you are telling a lie. Placing your hand on your chin and stretching your finger under your nose may also be interpreted as deceitful.

Stroking your chin is a sign of decision making.

Up in Arms

Crossing your arms or legs generally indicates something negative—either disapproval, disagreement, or dislike—and creates a barrier between you and your listener.

This "cross" behavior includes one arm across the chest, crossed ankles, and crossed legs. The ankle lock is an indication that the listener is mentally biting his lip.

Here are some ways to arrange your body in an open, welcoming posture:

- Uncross your arms and let them hang by your side, or place them behind your back.
- Open your palms as a further sign of your receptivity.
- Uncross your legs and feet and stand in a neutral position, feet slightly apart.
- Lean slightly forward with an attentive expression.

Exercise 7

How to Be Some "Body"

Start by noticing the body language you're using now. Pick a situation in the morning, one in the early afternoon, and a third in the late afternoon or evening and observe your posture and gestures. Then write down your natural tendencies, the way you most often sit and stand, as well as your favored listening position. As you observe yourself, write down small ways you can make your body an ice-breaking asset.

Morning

Describe the situation. _____

_____

Describe your positioning.

	____ Seated	____ Standing
Arm position:	____ Crossed	____ Behind back
	____ At your side	____ Gesturing
	____ Holding something	____ Other
Leg position:	____ Crossed	____ Uncrossed
Hand position:	____ Touching your face	

If so, how and where? _____

_____

___ Open Palm   ___ Clenched
___ Chin Stroking

Describe your facial expression. _____

_____

What is your body saying? _____

_____

_____

What do you want your body to say? _____

_____

_____

_____

Early Afternoon

Describe the situation. _____

_____

Describe your positioning.

	____ Seated	____ Standing
Arm position:	____ Crossed	____ Behind back
	____ At your side	____ Gesturing
	____ Holding something	____ Other
Leg position:	____ Crossed	____ Uncrossed
Hand position:	____ Touching your face	

If so, how and where? _____

_____

___ Open Palm   ___ Clenched
___ Chin Stroking

Describe your facial expression. _____

_____

What is your body saying? _____

_____

_____

What do you want your body to say? _____

_____

_____

_____

Late Afternoon or Evening

Describe the situation. _____

_____

Describe your positioning.

	____ Seated	____ Standing
Arm position:	____ Crossed	____ Behind back
	____ At your side	____ Gesturing
	____ Holding something	____ Other
Leg position:	____ Crossed	____ Uncrossed
Hand position:	____ Touching your face	

If so, how and where? _____

_____

___ Open Palm   ___ Clenched
___ Chin Stroking

Describe your facial expression. _____

_____

What is your body saying? _____

_____

_____

What do you want your body to say? _____

_____

_____

_____

Practice noticing your body language for two weeks. You'll learn how to remove unnecessary barriers between yourself and others. In ice-breaking situations, those barriers get in the way.

Use the body analysis you completed in Exercise 7 to notice how you are affected by your situation and time of day. What happens when you get hungry, tired, cold, or irritable?

Work on sitting and standing in positions of openness and acceptance. Notice how that makes you feel.

Now turn the chairs and look at the body language around you. Who looks open, and who has a dusty "Closed" sign in their window? Observe people in meetings and reception areas, during lunch, and in informal conversations. Watch for the kinds of people who have the most welcoming body works.

Things I Learned About Myself in This Chapter

1. _____

   _____

2. _____

   _____

3. _____

   _____

Things to Do to Improve My Ice-Breaking Skills

1. _____

   _____

2. _____

   _____

3. _____

Remember that your goal as you work through this book is to improve your on-the-spot communication skills — to turn unfamiliar or uncomfortable situations into business-building potential. Learning to read other people's body language and making yourself aware of your own puts you a step ahead. Read on to learn how to really melt some ice.

Chapter

Three

Lines That Melt the Ice

---

*"E*very encounter with another person is an opportunity to
make them like you and help you further your aims in life."

Barry Farber, *Making People Talk*

*Before going into the game, Kevin mentally suits up. He
knows the competition is fierce, the players intense. But
Kevin has been working out and he's ready. He adjusts
his clothing, carefully selected for its comfort. Mentally, he
arranges his tools, the tactics he's going to use to over-
whelm the opposition and win. Finally, he straightens his
tie and enters the meeting room.*

*The room is brightly lit, with tables of eight. Kevin
chooses a seat at a table already filled with five people.
No one is talking. Finally, a woman across the table
smiles and says, "How are you?" Kevin tries out his first
tactic.*

"I've been thinking about laughter this morning. Before I left for work, my daughter asked me, 'Dad why are you always so serious?' So I've been thinking about ways I can put more laughter into my life. I'd love some input."

Instantly the woman reaches into her purse and pulls out a set of jacks in a plastic carrying case. She hands them over to Kevin and says, "Try this."

People start to smile—the ice begins to melt. Kevin is on his way to having an interesting lunch, one that may even produce several valuable business contacts.

How often have you been trapped in one of those tepid interchanges that make you tap your foot, bite your lip, and look for ways to escape? Next time, instead of poking dead coals and expecting to start a flame, *be* the bright flame! Make it *your* responsibility to ignite the conversation by saying something interesting. Fascinating conversation doesn't just happen. It's an art form—and one that can ultimately reap wonderful business results.

By encouraging a stranger to talk to you, you are not only setting yourself up as a dynamic leader but also gathering information that could possibly help you in a later business situation.

Okay, so you're convinced that ice breaking is for you, but you're not quite sure how to best plunge in. In this chapter, you'll gather practical ways to start conversations that suit your personality and style. But first, take this quiz to see where your conversation openers need strengthening.

Exercise 8

Assessing Your Opening Lines

Circle the response that comes closest to how you'd react in each situation.

1. You've tossed aside your fears and worked on positive body language. You're ready to ice-break with the best of them. In the classroom where you're taking a night class, you notice a woman seated across the table from you. What do you say?

    A. "Isn't this weather discouraging?"

    B. "Boy, did I have a hard day."

    C. "That necklace is intriguing. Where did you find such a great piece of quartz?"

2. You're gearing yourself up to invite conversation. As a financial analyst, you want to carry something that will easily lead to mention of your field. Which of the following best suits you?

    A. A briefcase that's zebra-striped

    B. *Barron's* financial newspaper

    C. A button that says "Count on me"

3. You're talking up a storm—your new ice-breaking program is really working. Then you notice that your listener is staring off into space. What do you do?

    A. Talk louder

    B. Stop talking and see if she notices

    C. End the conversation and consider whether you talked too much

4. You've been standing in line for hours (it seems), and nobody has said a word to you. You're bored and restless. What do you do?

    A. Wait for some brave person to start a conversation

    B. Hum—and see whether anyone begins singing the words

    C. Smile and introduce yourself to the person behind you

In this quiz, the C answers are the "icebreakers." Now that you have a handle on the areas where you are strong, read on to learn about some tools for creating grand openings.

Ice-Breaking Tools

Find out what motivates people. Barry Farber, author of *Making People Talk,* says: "Imagine you are a broadcasting station. Everything you say is your own personal talk show. Watch newspapers, magazines, for what provokes, challenges, and interests others."

You are marketing a product—yourself. As with any marketing endeavor, you are asking, "What do people really want?" When you understand what motivates people, you can better direct the conversation and, thus, benefit from it.

Here are some typical motivators:

- Personal power
- Feeling important
- Recognition
- Social approval
- New experiences
- Love
- Emotional security

This list implies that people want to make a personal connection, to feel comfortable, and to be noticed. But what casual topics do most people use to break the ice? Weather, sports, and politics.

Instead of talking about the temperature and touchdowns, why not notice and praise people? Everyone wants to feel important and acknowledged. Ice breaking in this way is like handing someone a small bouquet of good feelings.

So "suit up." Delve into your own rich resources and create some fuel for ice breaking. Remember, facile conversation takes practice, openness, and a willingness to risk.

Notice details about people and your surroundings. If you can train yourself to notice the details about people and your surroundings, you'll greatly enhance your communication skills. Here are some things to look for:

- *People:* Unusual clothes, hats, shoes, jewelry, watches, name tags, briefcases, satchels, books, shopping bags, and body language (notice who has their "Open" sign out and who is "Closed")

- *Surroundings:* Art work, signage, sculpture, books, furniture, magazines, equipment, unusual floor or wall coverings

- *Social:* Food, the mix of people, the energy level, the size of the crowd, special guests or speakers, historical significance of the gathering spot

Now think about what else you have in common with the people around you. Besides the physical surroundings, what other topics could spark an interesting conversation?

- *Nostalgia:* Everyone likes to discuss good memories. Use the present to trigger people's memories of the past. This softens the conversation and puts it on a nonthreatening but personal plane.

- *Favorites:* Ask people about their favorite books, restaurants, movies, business seminars—you get the picture.

- *How to:* Everyone has tricks for getting the most out of life. Start a conversation by asking: How do you deal with stress? How do you find the best buy on FAX machines? How do you make the time to exercise?

- *Common ground:* Look at all the things you have in common with the people around you. Are you in the same building? Are you both drinking coffee? Are you standing in the same line? Find ways to turn these small similarities into worthwhile conversation.

You can also bring your own mixture of ice-breaking goodies with you.

Read my T-shirt... Wear or carry something that will provoke interest and comment.

- Dick always carries an interesting book with him when he goes into new situations.

   "People can't resist looking at what I'm reading," he says. "I often pick a current bestseller or a book with some controversy attached. This immediately invites conversations."

- Sarah carries her own coffee mug, so she won't have to use disposable cups. Her mug has a humorous message and gives her a chance to talk about her interest in ecology.

   "Everyone asks, 'Why are you carrying around a mug?'" Sarah says. "It's a great way to provoke interesting conversation."

- Barbara buys unusual clothes wherever she travels. A Mid-westerner, she dresses in bright clothes with a distinct Southwest flavor.

   "People often comment on the brilliant colors and designs in my clothes," Barbara says. "This leads to talk about colors and art, which allows me to talk about my framing business."

What can you wear or carry that will evoke conversation that works for you?

Be a leader. Someone has to be. When two people meet, the first person to establish communication is usually considered the leader. Project a confident image and people will assume you should be listened to.

When approaching a potential audience:

- Establish eye contact and exhibit pleasant, open body language.
- Use an interesting, provocative opening that's easy to understand.
- Adopt an encouraging attitude and welcoming listening skills.

Ask open-ended questions. In theatre, everyone wants to open in New York. But for your opening dialogue, you don't want the crowded tension of a city. You want to create a feeling of prairie—of wide, open places with lots of room for wandering and creative response. Devise open-ended questions that lend themselves to creative response. The more open your question, the more you can learn from the other person's answer. And the more places your subsequent response takes your listener, the better chance you have of building a conversation that will be memorable and mutually beneficial.

Often, brief interchanges are perfunctory. People toss out sentences thoughtlessly; they listen halfheartedly to answers.

Here are some examples of "crowded questions" that don't invite a creative response:

- Do you live around here?
- What line of work are you in?
- Is your name Swedish in origin?

All of these questions can by answered with one word. Notice how many of these crowded questions are hurled at you each day. As a master icebreaker, you want to avoid openers that your audience can handle with one word. Remember, you're not looking for the correct answer: you're looking for a connection.

Keep a file of interesting topics. National speakers say you need to GRAB your audience within the first ten seconds. How can you heighten the drama of your encounter? How can you GRAB with the right questions?

"I have a mental file of topics and questions that I use to initiate conversation," says Anne Baber, national speaker and co-author of the book *Great Connections*.

To create your own resource bank, you want timeless items that everyone could be interested in, tasty tidbits, hors d'oeuvres for the intellectually starving. Search for funny stories that don't go out of style, trends, book and restaurant reviews. Start a file of fascinating folks. Remember to concentrate on topics, not on gossip. Gossip can choke you, flood you out at the wrong moment.

Make a list of the topics you are interested in, topics that you know about from work, topics you want to know about, hobbies. Then select twenty of the topics that appeal most to you. These are the topics you can build files on. Watch for news articles, cartoons, television shows, pictures, anything that keeps your information lively and flowing.

Be creative in the way you add to your topic file. Consider these sources:

- Trivia collections
- Popular magazines
- Alternative presses, such as *Utne Reader,* that offer an excellent source of provocative articles
- National Public Radio
- Audiocassettes (Get them from the library and enrich your mind as you drive.)

Remember, your mind is the most important asset in your ice-breaking foray. Canned material loses its flavor if you can't directly adapt it to the situation.

Create grand openings out of what you are thinking at the moment. Your candid thoughts create a natural bridge into a personal conversation. For example:

- "This is my first financial seminar and I'm feeling over-whelmed. How do you ingest all the information?"
- "How did you get involved in your work?"
- "I've been feeling stressed lately. Do you have any tips on how to let go of tension?"
- "Your name is interesting. What's the story behind it?"

Creating great opening lines doesn't take a lot of work. Just by being alert, you'll notice information out there, ready and waiting for you.

Once you have a wealth of information, you're ready to create your own award-winning dialogue. You're writing an opening that gently demands more than a cursory "yes" or "no." You're creating dialogue that puts the listener in charge of the answer. He or she can either answer succinctly or offer extra tidbits to enrich and enliven the conversation and to further your encounter.

Use Exercise 9 to create your own grand openings.

Exercise 9

Creating Your Own Grand Openings

Get your audience involved and interested within the first ten seconds. Avoid questions they can dismiss with a "yes" or "no." Create a list of provocative questions that will give you many avenues for further plotting your conversations.

Grow your list for one week, adding five questions each day. The more openings you write down, the more spontaneous you will become at creating grand openings on the spur of the moment.

Day 1

1. _____
   _____

2. _____
   _____

3. _____
   _____

4. _____
   _____

5. _____
   _____

6. _____
   _____

7. _____
   _____

8. _____
   _____

9. _____
   _____

10. _____
    _____

Day 2

1. _____
   _____

2. _____
   _____

3. _____
   _____

4. _____
   _____

5. _____
   _____

Day 3

1. _____
   _____

2. _____
   _____

3. _____
   _____

4. _____
   _____

5. _____
   _____

Day 4

1. _____
   _____

2. _____
   _____

3. _____
   _____

4. _____
   _____

5. _____
   _____

Day 5

1. _____
   _____

2. _____
   _____

3. _____
   _____

4. _____
   _____

5. _____
   _____

Day 6

1. _____
   _____

2. _____
   _____

3. _____
   _____

4. _____
   _____

5. _____
   _____

Day 7

1. _____
   _____

2. _____
   _____

3. _____
   _____

4. _____
   _____

5. _____
   _____

Go With the "Floe" to Keep Conversations Moving

Now that you've learned several tools for opening conversations, here are some tips for keeping the conversation moving.

Prepare interesting answers. Sometimes people ask you stale questions. But you can be prepared with an interesting, off-beat answer, something that makes people stop the "talk" treadmill and pay attention to you. Anne Baber, co-author of *Great Connections*, makes the following suggestions for responding to inquiries about your job:

- "I make sure everything counts," a CPA might say.
- "I keep things cooking," a chef might answer.

Exercise 10

Creating Fiery Responses to Stale Questions

Make a list of the questions people ordinarily ask you. Include the "Hi, how are you's?" and "What do you do?" questions that pertain specifically to you and your work. Now have a mini brainstorming session with yourself. Ask yourself the question and write down any answer that comes to mind. Go quickly. Be sloppy. Get absurd. If you prefer, do this with friends and ask them to come up with wild answers. Now take those wild answers and tame them a bit. This will give you the provocative answers that make people listen to you and ask for more.

Question: _____

Answer: _____

"Tamed" Response: _____

Question: _____

Answer: _____

"Tamed" Response: _____

Question: _____
Answer: _____
"Tamed" Response: _____

Question: _____
Answer: _____
"Tamed" Response: _____

Question: _____
Answer: _____
"Tamed" Response: _____

Question: _____
Answer: _____
"Tamed" Response: _____

Question: _____
Answer: _____
"Tamed" Response: _____

Question: _____
Answer: _____
"Tamed" Response: _____

Question: _____
Answer: _____
"Tamed" Response: _____

Think of ways to make what you say unique. Create dialogue that characterizes you. Watch for interesting words you can sprinkle into your speech. Create your own picturesque clichés so that people will remember your words.

One way to do this is to play with metaphorical thinking. A metaphor is a figure of speech that contains a comparison of two dissimilar objects.

- "Playing cards is like shopping at a discount store: both depend on a really good deal."

- "Cooking is like throwing a javelin, because I never know where my efforts will end up."

Exercise 11

Practicing Metaphorical Thinking

Make a list of objects and actions and randomly join them together. Then see how they are similar. Do this alone or with a partner.

For example:

Rose	Cowboy hat
Necktie	Dancing to country music
Snowstorm	Stargazing
Riding a bike	Chocolate ice cream
Eating goulash	Rocking chair
Child	Tree

How is a rose like a rocking chair? How is riding a bike like dancing to country music? Stretch your mind and add sparkle to your ice-breaking efforts as you incorporate some unique metaphorical phrases into your conversation.

_____

_____

_____

_____

_____

_____

_____

_____

_____

_____

_____

Balance the information exchange. Make sure no one is doing *all* the talking.

Discuss topics important to you. Sincerity is a vital part of connecting with strangers. If you have a purely ulterior motive for talking to someone, that person will probably sense it and won't be as responsive to you.

Change topics and share information. Keep in mind what you have to offer, what you have to give to your listener.

Continue to seek out common interests and experiences. Just as seeking common ground is a tool for opening conversation, it is also a useful technique for developing a conversation. Listen for clues the other person may drop as the conversation progresses.

In a casual ice-breaking situation, you generally don't want to get too personal instantly. Establish a comfortable rapport and do get to know something about the person beyond the obvious.

Look for holes in the ice. Notice how people respond to what you're saying. If you're entertaining only yourself, revise your material. You're not there to babble on—you're there to draw the other person out.

Making a Graceful Exit

Leave your listener wanting more, not oversaturated. End your conversation by summing up what the other person has said and by saying how much you enjoyed the conversation.

Anne Baber suggests these three tips for a graceful exit:

1. *Sum up and appreciate.* Give the other person a synopsis of what you talked about and let him or her know how much the conversation enlightened and helped you.

2. *Explain the next step.* If you promised to exchange business cards and get together again, clarify that when you leave.

3. *Shake hands and leave.* It's the simplest way to part.

Now you're ready to march into any unknown territory, armed and conversational. As you do, remember to use this four-point ODES model:

Open your body language for your approach.

Deliver a wide-open and fast-paced grand opening.

Empathetically listen.

Share your ideas generously.

Things I Learned About Myself in This Chapter

1. _____

_____

2. _____

_____

3. _____

_____

Things to Do to Improve My Ice-Breaking Skills

1. _____

_____

2. _____

_____

3. _____

Now you've gathered several practical ways to start conversations that suit your personality and style. You've also learned techniques for sustaining conversations once you've broken the ice with your opening lines. You've moved one step closer to your goal of using on-the-spot communication to build business.

Chapter

Four

Listening
Is Hot

---

*C*arol was tense. In ten minutes, she would be *riding the elevator to the top floor of an exclusive Las Vegas hotel to present her company's jewelry products to a major client. She straightened her Elvis pin, one of the company's bestsellers, and dashed into the hotel gift shop for a package of breath mints. As she fumbled in her purse for a dollar, the clerk said: "I love your pin. I wish we had something like that in magnets."*

Carol stopped fumbling. She wasn't sure she'd heard correctly. "Can you tell me more about that?"

"We sell a lot of magnets," the clerk said. "If we had Elvis on a magnet, people would go wild."

Carol listened to every word and repeated the concept to herself. She asked the clerk for the number of magnets she guessed might sell every day. Then on a paper towel

*in the restroom, she mapped out a new proposal that
included selling magnets to the hotel's chain of gift shops.
Five minutes later she was presenting her new sales
pitch to a very interested client.*

Carol got a great idea from a few words. She might have missed
them.

Although we do more listening than anything besides breathing,
most of us retain only 25 percent of what we hear. That means
we miss, misinterpret, or misunderstand 75 percent of all that
we hear. Test *your* listening skills with Exercise 12.

Exercise 12

Listen Up!

1. The woman who sits down next to you on the bus begins to talk to you. She pours out a poignant story about her fifteen-year-old-daughter, who is threatening to run away unless she gets to visit her boyfriend at college. "I'm absolutely at my wit's end," the woman says.

   What do you say?

   A. "You wouldn't believe what happened to me when my daughter was that age."

   B. "If I were you, I'd see a family therapist together."

   C. "It sounds like you're having a terrible time with this. Tell me more."

2. You are annoyed that you have to shepherd the copy repairperson around the office. You impatiently bend paper clips while the machine is being serviced. "If you work with the throttle and adjust the toner a quarter of an inch next time, you can easily fix the machine yourself," he says. You are thinking about what you're going to have for lunch and don't quite hear him.

   What do you say?

   A. Nothing. Bend another paper clip and envision a plate of moo goo gai pan.

   B. "That's fine. Thanks for fixing it. I'll show you to the elevator."

   C. "Could you repeat what you said about the throttle? I want to write that down so I can remember it."

3. While you're waiting for a project at the copy center, you sit next to a woman who tells you her name and her place of business. You've been wanting a contact at that particular business. Your order is ready and you prepare to end your encounter. But you can't remember her name.

What do you do?

   A. Get a good look at her so you can describe her to the receptionist at that company.

   B. Hope you remember her name later.

   C. Ask for her business card and vow to pay attention the next time you hear someone's name.

The "C" answers mean you are closer to your goal of improving ice-breaking skills through active listening.

Active Listening

You've had an experience like this. Perhaps you're talking to your teenage daughter, perhaps you're placing an order with a waitress who's had a hard day. You look at the person and speak earnestly, but the person is gazing away from you, seemingly indifferent. Have you been heard? What is your clue that your teenager heard her curfew and will be home on time? How can you know you'll get French fries instead of mashed potatoes?

A big part of listening is acknowledging. Remember from Chapter 3 that one of the prime motivators is recognition. Listening is a chance to actively recognize another person, without even using your brilliant conversational skills.

Here are some tips for active listening:

1. Sit or stand with an open, accepting posture.

2. Look at the speaker, or if eye contact is too intense, look at the bridge of the speaker's nose.

3. Stand straight.

4. When the speaker says something, ask for more information. This shows your interest.

5. Center your questions on the speaker: "Do you think...?" "Would you advise?" "Tell me more about..." Don't steal the conversation.

6. Respond to the speaker. After the person shares information with you, repeat something you heard.

Listening Leverage

Think about your normal listening situations: one-on-one conversations, meetings, seminars, family situations, social settings. When is it hard for you to pay attention? When is it easy? What sorts of things do you typically forget about a person? What do you always remember?

How much you actually hear can give you leverage with the other person.

Filling out Exercise 13 will help you to recognize listening situations that are ideal for you and those that are challenging. Use what you learn to improve your listening skills and gain leverage with others.

Exercise 13

How Much Listening Leverage Do I Have?

Think of an ideal situation — one where your listening skills are at their best. Describe the situation so that you can recreate it in your ice-breaking forays.

Then describe a situation in which listening is difficult for you. By acknowledging your listening challenges, you'll be alert to possible danger situations.

Your ideal listening situation:

Environment _____

_____

_____

Number of people _____

_____

_____

Setting _____

_____

_____

_____

Duration _____

_____

_____

_____

Purpose of listening _____

_____

_____

_____

Your difficult listening situation:

Environment _____

_____

_____

Number of people _____

_____

_____

Setting _____

_____

_____

_____

Duration _____

_____

_____

_____

Purpose of listening _____

_____

_____

_____

Mastering the Message

Listening is a productivity tool—when you know how to listen, you can understand problems better, retain more information, and create better working relationships.

When you really listen, people think you're smart.

When you're actively listening, you are participating. Listening is an active, integrated communication skill that demands energy and know-how.

To listen effectively, you must hear and select information, give it meaning, determine how you feel about it, and respond, all in a matter of seconds.

You must understand the speaker's purpose, which could be entertaining, persuading, sharing feelings, making small talk. For each purpose, you listen differently.

Listening unlocks ice-breaking resistance. Here are the four keys to opening this door:

1. *Hear the message.* Tune out distractions.

   Repeat or clarify. Say: "This is how I understand what you're saying. Am I correct?"

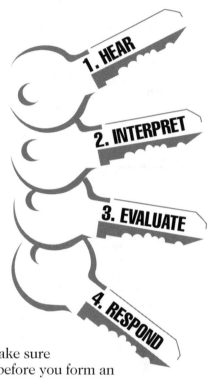

2. *Interpret the message.* Do this by tuning in to the speaker's words, tone of voice, nonverbal clues. Often personal emotional filters get in the way of a correct interpretation of the message. Be aware of memories, perceptions, emotional hot buttons, and attitudes that make you subjective.

3. *Evaluate the message.* Ask questions; analyze evidence. Don't jump to conclusions: Make sure you have all the information before you form an opinion.

4. *Respond to the speaker.* Let the speaker know you heard. This completes the communication process. Your response informs the speaker that you heard the message and understood and evaluated it appropriately. The response helps you to reach a common understanding, give feedback, and avoid confusion.

Listening Locks

Even when you have good intentions, if you aren't diligent about listening, it's easy to get "listening locks."

Daydreaming, interrupting, jumping to conclusions, and stealing the conversation all interrupt and disturb listening.

Here are some ways to improve your listening skills:

Before and after. Listen now; report later. Think of someone you can share the information with. This will improve your interest and your retention.

Ready, aim, focus! Try to stay focused by repeating to yourself portions of the speaker's message.

User-friendly. Learn to want to listen. Think of how the information will benefit you and how you can use it.

Pull off listening leeches. Watch out for these listening leeches:

- You're in a hurry.
- You're distracted by things going on around you.
- You're bored.
- You're thinking about what you're going to say next.
- You're in surroundings that are out of your comfort zone.
- You feel that you already know what the speaker is going to say.
- You're stressed out and on mental overload.
- You're tired.

When you notice an attack of listening leeches, try to refocus, recenter. Change your position, your expression. Ask a pertinent question. Enhance your open body language so you feel more a part of the conversation.

Button up. Control emotional hot buttons. There are probably certain words, phrases, and mannerisms that bother you. When you feel unsettled by another person's communication method, try responding in one of these ways:

- Take a deep breath.
- Ask questions for clarification.
- Try to see the other person's viewpoint.
- Be patient.

Exercise 14

Pulling Off Listening Leeches

Each of the following experiences involves a listening challenge. What gets in the way of fully listening to the speaker? What can you do to get rid of those listening leeches?

1. You're late for lunch. You're standing in line at a popular food stand in the middle of a noisy mall. The man behind you starts a conversation. What could detract you from listening and what can you do to solve the problem?

   Listening Leeches: _____

   _____

   _____

   _____

   Solving the Problem: _____

   _____

   _____

   _____

2. You're being escorted to a potential banquet suite by the meeting planner connected with the hotel. "Dear," he says, "you'll love this room." Your ex-spouse used to call you "dear."

   Listening Leeches: _____

   _____

   _____

   _____

   Solving the Problem: _____

   _____

   _____

   _____

3. You're saving a seat for a friend at a seminar. You begin a conversation with the woman on the next aisle. The speaker is testing the microphone. You're worried that your friend is going to be late.

Listening Leeches: _____

_____

_____

_____

Solving the Problem: _____

_____

_____

_____

Remember, active listening is just as important a part of communicating as delivering a grand opening line. If you listen closely, you'll pick up clues from the other person that you can use to keep the conversation moving.

Things I Learned About Myself in This Chapter

_1._ _____

_____

_2._ _____

_____

_3._ _____

_____

 Things to Do to Improve My Ice-Breaking Skills

_1._ _____

_____

_2._ _____

_____

_3._ _____

Now that you know how to capitalize on your listening skills, you're ready to battle rejection with elegance. Learn how in Chapter 5.

Chapter

Five

Iceberg Alert:
How to Deal With Indifference or Rejection

---

*G*eorge *is late for an important meeting. He simply
can't find the address he has written down. Feeling
desperate, he squeezes his car into the only clear spot on
the street and heads towards a group of three people
clustered outside a prestigious-looking building.*

*He lingers hopefully, waiting for someone to acknowledge
him. Finally, he says: "Excuse me. I'm a stranger and I'm
feeling stranger because I'm lost."*

*He's greeted with three deadpan faces. No one smiles. No
one offers advice or direction.*

*George shrugs and then notices a man sitting at a
nearby bus stop, working away with a calculator
and spreadsheet.*

"Excuse me," George says. "I'm trying for the lost and found. I'm the lost one."

The man listens to George's dilemma and directs him to the correct building (which is right in front of him).

"Who are you seeing?" the man asks.

When George tells him, the man says: "I like a man who admits when he's lost. Use my name. Say Byron recommended you."

George rushes to his meeting. Using Byron's name not only smoothes over his lateness, but also impresses the potential client.

Rejection is a part of ice breaking. As a master of on-the-spot communication, you will meet people who are sullen, uncommunicative, and just don't want to deal with you. So how do you deal with *them?* See how well you handle these situations by taking the following quiz.

Exercise 15

How Well Do I Handle Icebergs?

1. Every Friday your office has casual dress day. Every Friday you take the stairs to the seventh floor instead of the elevator. This is the third week that a woman wearing a Harley T-shirt and jeans has been walking the stairs at the same time you are. You are ready with your ice-breaking strategy: "Your T-shirt reminds me of the summer I rode a motorcycle to Colorado. Have you done any long-distance traveling on a motorcycle?" The woman looks at you like you have fudge smeared all over your nose. What do you do?

   A. Say "Oops, sorry," and run up the rest of the stairs.

   B. Wait out the silence until she answers. If she doesn't answer, say "Have a good day."

   C. Say: "I asked you a question. I'd really appreciate an answer."

2. You have successfully conquered your fear of approaching strangers and are talking to the man next to you in the postal line. He's in the middle of discussing his strategy for minimizing mailing costs, when he suddenly stops talking and walks away. You are astonished. You think:

   A. "Maybe I wasn't a good enough listener."

   B. "This man has a problem with manners."

   C. "I'll never talk to another stranger."

3. You're in a crowded lunch meeting and sit down at an almost full table for eight. You compliment the man on your right on his unusual carrying case and ask the story behind it. He begins, his eyes shining. Then right in the middle of his story about his trip to Persia, he begins a

conversation with the woman on the other side of him, leaving you with no one to talk to. What do you think?

A. "Perhaps asking about his carrying case was too sensitive a subject."

B. "I'll talk to the people across the table and maybe have better luck."

C. "Maybe I'm putting my foot in my mouth. I better clam up."

If you answered with "B"s, you have the self-esteem that "tough-world" on-the-spot conversation requires.

A Matter of Survival

"Ice breaking is a survival-based activity," says Paul Anderson, Ph.D., a psychologist in private practice.

Like the primates, who have social networks essential for survival, humans also depend on a social network. The roles that we assume satisfy socially created needs rather than biologically created needs. This brings in territorial battles and issues of control that make us fearful.

"People often think, 'If I get too much rejection, I'll be on the periphery of the social network, and my survival chances go down,'" says Dr. Anderson.

He continues: "Ice breaking is a combat zone for win-lose. The more you stay out of the battle mentality, the better you'll be able to handle rejection when it comes."

The secret is to keep your ego from becoming involved. Tell yourself: "This (the rejection) is not personal. These people don't even really know me."

Here are some winning ways to approach each new situation:

Fear is okay. Be aware of your fear and manage it.

Think of each situation as teamwork. You are forming a new team made up of you and the person you approach.

Refuse to make rejection your problem. If some people are rude to you, that's their problem. Don't let your self-esteem be smashed by thoughtless communicators.

Notice body language. Avoid people whose body language is sending out a "closed, hostile" message.

Remember, rejection is about the *other* person, not about you.

Exercise 16

Rebuilding the Titanic

Even the great communicators have rotten moments.
Analyzing the situation afterwards helps you learn. Think of a
situation in which your conversational overtures were
rejected. Describe it here.

1. Describe the situation.

_____

_____

_____

_____

2. Describe the listener's response.

_____

_____

_____

_____

3. How did you feel?

_____

_____

_____

_____

4. What would you do differently next time?

_____

_____

_____

_____

Things I Learned About Myself in This Chapter

1. _____

_____

2. _____

_____

3. _____

_____

Things to Do to Improve My Ice-Breaking Skills

1. _____

_____

2. _____

_____

3. _____

Now that you are tough stuff, you're ready to turn your waits into wonders.

Chapter

Six

Ice-Break While You Wait

"*H*ave *a wonderful flight," the flight attendant said, as Ruth settled into her first-class seat. After a grueling week of presenting training seminars, Ruth's plane had been delayed. She hoped her seatmate would be pleasant. As she pulled out a notebook and began preparing for the next day's speech, her seatmate rushed in, stepping on her foot and poking her in the ribs as he buckled his seat belt.*

Ruth looked up from her work and smiled at him. "Forgive me for being so busy," she said. "I'm just swamped with work, and trying to make the most of every moment."

"What are you working on?" he asked.

Ruth told him about her training programs and described the new one she was developing.

"You're just the kind of person we need to present at our national convention," the man said.

During the next two years, Ruth not only presented at the national convention but also made audiotapes for the group and gave several training programs.

How can you turn those periods of waiting into "heavyweight" business connections? Explore this situational series and see how you would handle things.

The Ups and Downs of Elevator Ice Breaking

Waiting for the elevator gives you a nice opportunity to practice the "ice pick"—a quick icebreaker that gives the other person a glow and makes you feel good too.

The scene: You are standing by the "Up" button with another person. He pressed, you pressed, nothing's happening. At any moment, the elevator could appear. Yet the seconds crawl by, and you're still standing and standing still.

Strategy #1: This is a perfect time to notice something about the other person's appearance and make a comment or give a compliment. It's quick and it's fun. Most important, you are keying in on two of the people motivators you learned about in Chapter 3: recognition and approval.

For example: "I'm fascinated by your tie. Where did you find such a distinctive pattern?"

Strategy #2: Be prepared with a few "grand opening" icebreakers in your repertoire just in case the person is cased in gray with no distinguishing accessories. Here are a few examples:

- "What's the longest amount of time you've ever had to wait for an elevator?"

- "What do you do to relax yourself when you start feeling anxious about waiting?"

- "I've seen some great movies that have elevator scenes. What movies come to your mind?" (A question like this could produce either a lively conversation or silence. But ask it anyway if the mood seems high. Just have your own movie anecdotes ready to share.)

Your own grand opening: _____

_____

_____

_____

Making the Big Chill the Little Shiver: Reception Areas

The reception area is an important place for two types of ice-breaking situations: one with the receptionist and another with the people who are waiting with you. Your goal with the receptionist is to establish rapport, to make that person feel important and comfortable with you. Your goal for your fellow waitees is to keep yourself at ease while you're waiting, to make business contacts, and to make them feel recognized.

The scene: You are sitting in a chair in the reception area. The receptionist has told you it will be about ten minutes until your contact is ready to see you. The receptionist's desk has a number of objects on it: a vase of daisies, a picture of a girl wearing roller skates, a can of diet cola, a plastic cricket, and the usual office equipment. A serious-looking man, briefcase poised on his lap, *Wall Street Journal* in his hands, is seated. The company's annual report and newsletter and the local business journal are the reading material. The walls are adorned with grasscloth and several awards you can't quite read.

Strategy #1:

With the receptionist: Use the surrounding environment to open a conversation. If the receptionist doesn't seem harried, ask her a genuine question about something on her desk. Pick something that looks innocuous, yet interesting.

- "That cricket on your desk is interesting. Do you have time to tell me the story behind it?"

- "I notice this picture with the roller skates. My daughter's dying to roller skate, but can't seem to get the hang of it. What's the secret to getting started?"

With your fellow waitees: Watch their body language for signs of openness. Again, the environment can provide you with cues for beginning a conversation. The periodicals and the awards on the wall offer potential for breaking the ice. This is also a situation where your on-the-spot thoughts could create an effective opening. Here are some examples:

- "Which part of the *Journal* do you find most valuable?"
- "How did you get introduced to this company?"
- "Why do you think they chose such a bright purple for this annual report?"

Strategy #2: Keep a few "grand opening" icebreakers in your repertoire in case he hides behind his newspaper.

- "I heard an interesting statistic on the radio today. Did you know that listening is second only to breathing in how much of our time it takes up? What do you think of that?"
- "I've already spent an hour waiting in reception areas today. Fortunately, one of them was The Ritz, one of my favorite places. Do you have any favorite places to be caught waiting?"

Your own grand opening: _____

_____

_____

_____

Melting the Tension
Before the Meeting Starts

While waiting for a meeting to begin, use your ice-breaking skills to start the creative energies moving, to release tensions, and to increase communications. When you ice-break before a meeting, you develop a sense of camaraderie and trust that enhances the meeting. This is a good time to use the people motivators discussed in Chapter 3. Find openers that build on a person's esteem, importance, and recognition.

The scene: A few people are gathered around the massive conference table, but there is no conversation. It's a vendors' meeting and none of you know each other. You may even be competitors! No one wears a name tag. There's a mixture of men and women. The room is chilly and there's a sideboard with coffee and doughnuts. The carpet is thick and the chairs are hard to move. There isn't much mingling space. A few people are clustered in the coffee area.

Strategy #1: This is a good time to motivate people by making them feel recognized and important. This will lower tension and open the conversational channels. The coffee area is a good place to start. Food is a natural low-key, non-business-oriented conversation opener. After pouring yourself a cup of coffee and using open body language and a greeting, you might say:

- "It's unusual to call a meeting of vendors. What do you provide to the company?"

- "Anytime I'm in a new group of people, I feel a little nervous. What helps you look so at ease?"

You're giving your listeners a chance to feel important by recognizing them and asking for their advice.

Strategy #2: Think about what all these vendors have in common.

- "I recently read that small companies are increasingly involved in new product development. How do you think that will affect us?"

- "I find it unusual for a client to gather vendors together. Have any of your other clients ever called a meeting like this?"

Your own grand opening: _____

_____

_____

_____

Warming Up a Luncheon Meeting

Settings where food is served are natural places of bonding and comfort. The sooner you set the stage for camaraderie and fun, the more effective your luncheon experience will be.

The scene: The large room is filled with tables for six. The room is carpeted, sterile, and chilly. A salad and rolls already grace the table. At the far corner of the room, there's a lectern, and a technician is adjusting a large screen and a video monitor.

Strategy #1: This is a good way to let nostalgia open you to pleasant and possibly meaningful conversations. You have the time to talk more freely in this situation because you have 20 or

30 minutes before the speeches start. Pick a table with at least three or four people. Two people may be deep into an exclusive conversation. One person leaves more room for conversational doldrums. This is a good time to engage the entire group through a reminiscence.

- "Um-m-m. That meatloaf smell reminds me of my favorite lunch in the school cafeteria. What were your favorite lunches when you were a kid?"
- "These white tablecloths remind me of those endless Sunday dinners our family went to at my Aunt Louise's. Do you remember going places as a kid you didn't really want to go to?"
- "The television monitor reminds me of a psychology class I took. Three hundred people watched a video of the professor. What experiences have you had with learning from videos?"

Strategy #2: Think of your common ground. You are eating lunch together, attracted by the speaker, at the same tables, served by the same waitperson.

- "I like the idea of learning something while I eat. What other lunchtime programs have you found worthwhile?"
- "I'm thinking this speaker will really motivate me. What experience have any of you had with him before?"
- "I've heard that this hotel has an incredible pastry chef on staff. What experiences have you had with the food here?""

Your own grand opening: _____

_____

_____

_____

Ice Breaking While Waiting in Line

Be a line leader. People usually are ripe for conversation when they're waiting. Your goal is to break the monotony, to establish yourself as a dynamic leader. This is a chance to break ice with more than one person and create a group energy.

The scene: You are standing in line for a seminar featuring a well-known motivational speaker. The seating is open and the doors are still closed. You are in the middle of a ragged line of about thirty business people. To your left is a table with a selection of the speaker's books and videos. To your right is a table with coffee and water. In front of you is a woman with extremely high heels. She's draped a trenchcoat over her arm and its belt is dragging on the floor. Behind you is a man tapping his foot, his mouth in a tight line.

Strategy #1: This a good time to capitalize on common experience. Everyone in the line has sidestepped a busy day to hear this speaker. Find out why.

- "I've heard that the speaker's book on creative thinking is wonderful. Which of her books have you read?"

- "The speaker's team-building video made a big impact on me. I'm curious — what books do you feel are "must-reads" for business people?"

Strategy #2: Use the shared experience of waiting to pull you together, through a combination of discussion and nostalgia.

- "This is the best-dressed line I've stood in in quite a while. Last weekend, I stood in line with my son for rock concert tickets. Have you ever stood in line for hours?"

- "A friend of mine does yoga postures whenever she has to stand in line. She says it relaxes her. What tricks do you have for making the most out of line-standing?"

Your own grand opening: _____

_____

_____

_____

Exercise 17

Your Own Ice-Breaking Situation and Solution

Choose an ice-breaking situation that you encounter frequently but feel uncomfortable in. Then create your own solution.

1. What are your ice-breaking goals? _____

    _____

    _____

    _____

2. Write down the situation. This helps you problem solve.

    The scene: _____

    _____

    _____

3. Once you understand the dynamics of the scene, choose the ice-breaking strategy that seems most natural.

    Strategy #1: _____

    _____

    _____

    _____

    Strategy #2 (Consider alternatives): _____

    _____

    _____

    _____

4. Now create an opening line that is absolutely unique to you, something that echoes your personal style.

    Your own grand opening: _____

    _____

    _____

    _____

**Things I Learned About
Myself in This Chapter**

1. _____

_____

2. _____

_____

3. _____

_____

 **Things to Do to Improve
My Ice-Breaking Skills**

1. _____

_____

2. _____

_____

3. _____

You're now an on-the-spot conversational swimmer. To keep
your ice-breaking energy going, maintain a journal (see the
Sample Log Sheet on page 77). Briefly record your encounters,
with the contact name and date. Make it your goal to ice-break
several times each week, if not daily. And watch your
confidence, your communication skills, and your business grow.

Ice-Breaking and Business-Building Journal

Sample Log Sheet

Date _____

Situation _____

_____

_____

_____

Your Grand Opening _____

_____

_____

_____

Contact Name _____

Results of Connection:

❏ Pleasant, But No Promises

❏ Exchanged Business Cards

❏ Arranged to Meet Again

❏ Promised to Send Follow-through Information

Additional Comments _____

_____

_____

_____

_____

_____

BIBLIOGRAPHY AND SUGGESTED READING

Baber, Anne, and Lynne Wayman. *Great Connections: Small Talk and Networking for Businesspeople.* Manassas Park, VA: Impact Publications, 1992.

Clarke, Colleen S. *Networking: How to Creatively Tap Your People Resources.* Mission, KS: SkillPath Publications, 1993.

Farber, Barry. *Making People Talk.*

Pease, Allan. *Signals.* New York: Bantam Books, 1984.

Siress, Ruth, Deborah Shouse, and Carolyn Riddle. *A Working Woman's Communication Survival Guide.* New York: Prentice Hall, 1994.

Van Fleet, James K. *Lifetime Conversation Guide.* New York: Prentice Hall, 1986.

AVAILABLE FROM SKILLPATH PUBLICATIONS

Self-Study Sourcebooks

Climbing the Corporate Ladder: What You Need to Know and Do to Be a Promotable Person *by Barbara Pachter and Marjorie Brody*

Coping With Supervisory Nightmares: 12 Common Nightmares of Leadership and What You Can Do About Them *by Michael and Deborah Singer Dobson*

Defeating Procrastination: 52 Fail-Safe Tips for Keeping Time on Your Side *by Marlene Caroselli, Ed.D.*

Discovering Your Purpose *by Ivy Haley*

Going for the Gold: Winning the Gold Medal for Financial Independence *by Lesley D. Bissett, CFP*

Having Something to Say When You Have to Say Something: The Art of Organizing Your Presentation *by Randy Horn*

Info-Flood: How to Swim in a Sea of Information Without Going Under *by Marlene Caroselli, Ed.D.*

The Innovative Secretary *by Marlene Caroselli, Ed.D.*

Letters & Memos: Just Like That! *by Dave Davies*

Mastering the Art of Communication: Your Keys to Developing a More Effective Personal Style *by Michelle Fairfield Poley*

Obstacle Illusions: Coverting Crisis to Opportunity *by Marlene Caroselli, Ed.D.*

Organized for Success! 95 Tips for Taking Control of Your Time, Your Space, and Your Life *by Nanci McGraw*

A Passion to Lead! How to Develop Your Natural Leadership Ability *by Michael Plumstead*

P.E.R.S.U.A.D.E.: Communication Strategies That Move People to Action *by Marlene Caroselli, Ed.D.*

Productivity Power: 250 Great Ideas for Being More Productive *by Jim Temme*

Promoting Yourself: 50 Ways to Increase Your Prestige, Power, and Paycheck *by Marlene Caroselli, Ed.D.*

Proof Positive: How to Find Errors Before They Embarrass You *by Karen L. Anderson*

Risk-Taking: 50 Ways to Turn Risks Into Rewards *by Marlene Caroselli, Ed.D. and David Harris*

Stress Control: How You Can Find Relief From Life's Daily Stress *by Steve Bell*

The Technical Writer's Guide *by Robert McGraw*

Total Quality Customer Service: How to Make It Your Way of Life *by Jim Temme*

Write It Right! A Guide for Clear and Correct Writing *by Richard Andersen and Helene Hinis*

Your Total Communication Image *by Janet Signe Olson, Ph.D.*

Handbooks

The ABC's of Empowered Teams: Building Blocks for Success *by Mark Towers*

Assert Yourself! Developing Power-Packed Communication Skills to Make Your Points Clearly, Confidently, and Persuasively *by Lisa Contini*

Breaking the Ice: How to Improve Your On-the-Spot Communication Skills
by Deborah Shouse

The Care and Keeping of Customers: A Treasury of Facts, Tips, and Proven Techniques for Keeping Your Customers Coming BACK! *by Roy Lantz*

Challenging Change: Five Steps for Dealing With Change *by Holly DeForest and Mary Steinberg*

Dynamic Delegation: A Manager's Guide for Active Empowerment *by Mark Towers*

Every Woman's Guide to Career Success *by Denise M. Dudley*

Exploring Personality Styles: A Guide for Better Understanding Yourself and Your Colleagues *by Michael Dobson*

Grammar? No Problem! *by Dave Davies*

Great Openings and Closings: 28 Ways to Launch and Land Your Presentations With Punch, Power, and Pizazz *by Mari Pat Varga*

Hiring and Firing: What Every Manager Needs to Know *by Marlene Caroselli, Ed.D. with Laura Wyeth, Ms.Ed.*

How to Be a More Effective Group Communicator: Finding Your Role and Boosting Your Confidence in Group Situations *by Deborah Shouse*

How to Deal With Difficult People *by Paul Friedman*

Learning to Laugh at Work: The Power of Humor in the Workplace
by Robert McGraw

Making Your Mark: How to Develop a Personal Marketing Plan for Becoming More Visible and More Appreciated at Work *by Deborah Shouse*

Meetings That Work *by Marlene Caroselli, Ed.D.*

The Mentoring Advantage: How to Help Your Career Soar to New Heights
by Pam Grout

Minding Your Business Manners: Etiquette Tips for Presenting Yourself Professionally in Every Business Situation *by Marjorie Brody and Barbara Pachter*

Misspeller's Guide *by Joel and Ruth Schroeder*

Motivation in the Workplace: How to Motivate Workers to Peak Performance and Productivity *by Barbara Fielder*

NameTags Plus: Games You Can Play When People Don't Know What to Say
by Deborah Shouse

Networking: How to Creatively Tap Your People Resources *by Colleen Clarke*

New & Improved! 25 Ways to Be More Creative and More Effective *by Pam Grout*

Power Write! A Practical Guide to Words That Work *by Helene Hinis*

The Power of Positivity: Eighty ways to energize your life *by Joel and Ruth Schroeder*

Putting Anger to Work For You *by Ruth and Joel Schroeder*

Reinventing Your Self: 28 Strategies for Coping With Change *by Mark Towers*

Saying "No" to Negativity: How to Manage Negativity in Yourself, Your Boss, and Your Co-Workers *by Zoie Kaye*

The Supervisor's Guide: The Everyday Guide to Coordinating People and Tasks
by Jerry Brown and Denise Dudley, Ph.D.

Taking Charge: A Personal Guide to Managing Projects and Priorities
by Michal E. Feder

Treasure Hunt: 10 Stepping Stones to a New and More Confident You! *by Pam Grout*

A Winning Attitude: How to Develop Your Most Important Asset!
by Michelle Fairfield Poley

For more information, call 1-800-873-7545.